Contents

Math

Science

Reading Readiness

And More...

Visiting the Animals

Follow the numbers from 1 to 9.
Draw a line on the path.

Pond

Chicken Coop

Vegetable Garden

FARM FUNNIES
What keys won't open doors?

Turkeys!

Pig Pen

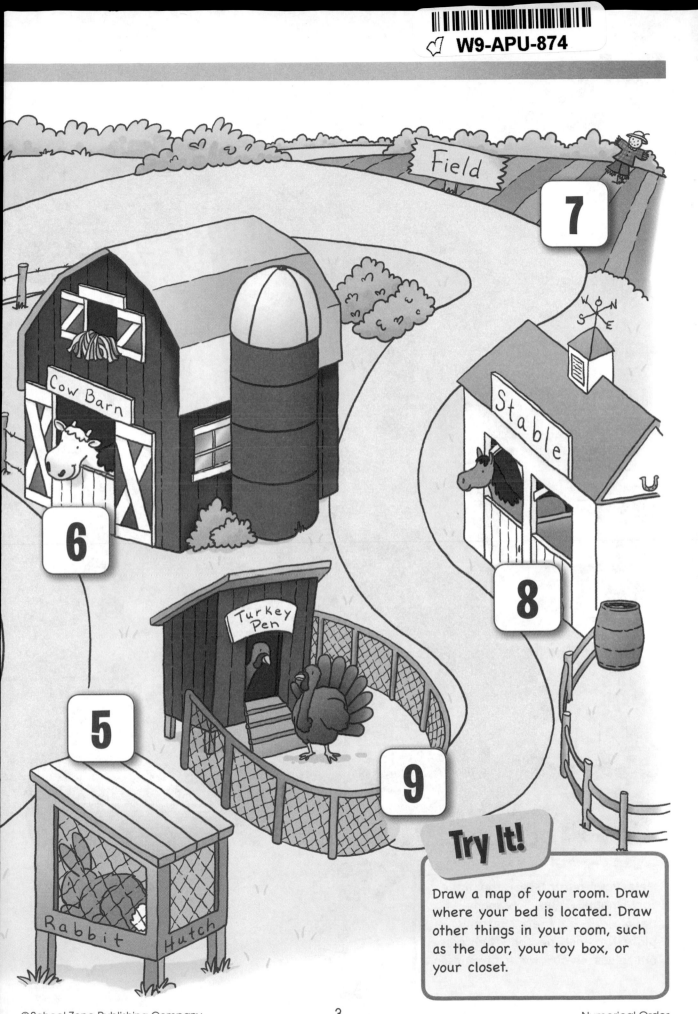

Try It!

Draw a map of your room. Draw where your bed is located. Draw other things in your room, such as the door, your toy box, or your closet.

Numerical Order

The Farm

1

one

Circle 1 👦.

Circle 1 🐔.

Circle 1 🚜.

Try It!

Help your parents set the table for a meal. Count how many people will be there. Set one plate for each person. Then place one glass or cup for each person.

The Cow Barn

2
two

Circle 2 s.

Circle 2 s.

Circle 2 s.

FARM FUNNIES

Why did the farmer feed his cow money?

He wanted rich milk!

Counting Two

The Garden

3
three

Circle 3 s.
Circle 3 s.
Circle 3 s.

Try It!

Does your family have a garden?
How is your garden the same as
a farm? How is it different?

Garden Giants

This 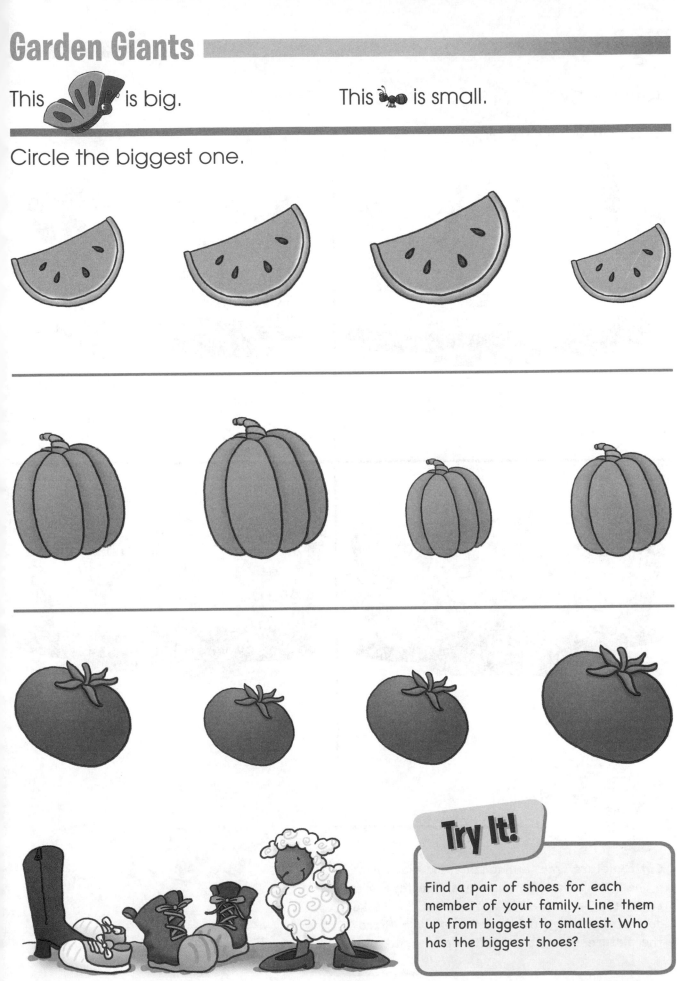 is big.   This 🐜 is small.

Circle the biggest one.

Try It!

Find a pair of shoes for each member of your family. Line them up from biggest to smallest. Who has the biggest shoes?

Size Differentiation

Pig Pens

How many 🐷s do you see?

Circle the number.

1 2 3

1 2 3

1 2 3

1 2 3

Try It!

Cut a picture from a magazine and place it on a sheet of paper. You might want to tape the edges of the picture to keep it in place. Make dots around the outside of the picture. Remove the picture. Now it's a dot-to-dot!

8

Around the Bend

This  is a circle.

Color two circles **blue**.

9

Circles

FARM FUNNIES

What do you call a crate of ducks?

A box of quackers!

Ducks

What Goes Together?

🐕 goes with 🦴.

Circle the picture that goes with the first one.

Try It!

How many ways can you sort your toy animals? Try sorting them by size and color. Then try dividing the animals into zoo and farm animals, wild animals and pets, furry animals and feathered ones, and so on.

Which One Is Different?

These  are the same. This is different.

Circle the picture that is different.

Same or Different

FARM FUNNIES

How do pigs write?

_____

With a pig pen!

Barnyard Colors

Color the pictures.

FARM FUNNIES • FARM FUNNIES • FARM FUNNIES

Why do cows wear bells?

Because their horns don't work!

Try It!

What is your favorite color? Try to find as many things as you can that are that color. Cut out pictures from a magazine, look in your refrigerator, and find clothes in your closet.

Colors

Finding the Ducklings

Draw a line to help the duck reach her ducklings.

Try It!

Stand quietly and try to hear as many sounds as you can. Then cup your hands behind your ears. Notice that things sound louder. Many animals have better hearing than people because their ears are shaped to collect sounds.

Sounding It Out

Say the names of the pictures.
Circle the picture whose name begins with the same sound as the first one.

A apple

B barn

C carrot

D dog

Try It!

Draw a large boat. Write A, B, C, and D on the boat. Cut out pictures of things whose names begin with each of the letters, and then glue the pictures to the boat.

The Field

4 ∷
four

Circle 4 s.

Circle 4 s.

Circle 4 s.

Try It!

Make up a song without using any words. Clap your hands, stomp your feet, and snap your fingers!

The Stable

5 ⁙
five

Circle 5 s.

Circle 5 ∩s.

Circle 5 🐭s.

FEED

FARM FUNNIES
What animal always goes to bed with its shoes on?

A horse!

The Farm House

6

:::

six

Circle 6 ⬭s.

Circle 6 ⊔s.

Try It!

You can make a funny-face snack. Cut a slice of bread into a circle. Cover it with peanut butter. Make a face using carrot curls, nuts, cheese, apples, or raisins for the eyes, ears, nose, and mouth.

18

Square Dance

This ▢ is a square.

Color two squares **red**.

Try It!

Choose one shape, such as a circle, square, triangle, or rectangle. Create a picture using only that shape. Then count how many times you used the shape in your drawing.

What Does Not Belong?

The 🍦 does not belong.

Circle the picture that does not belong.

FARM FUNNIES

What kind of vegetable goes "ding-dong"?

A bell pepper!

The Picnic

Circle how many there are.

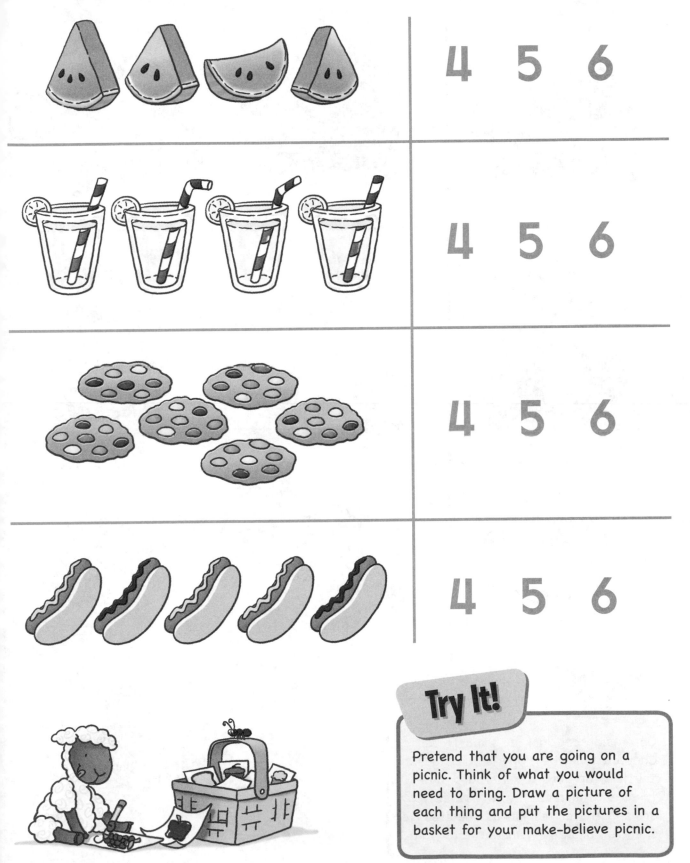

	4	5	6
	4	5	6
	4	5	6
	4	5	6

Try It!

Pretend that you are going on a picnic. Think of what you would need to bring. Draw a picture of each thing and put the pictures in a basket for your make-believe picnic.

Pond Friends

Circle the picture that is bigger than the first one.

Try It!

Go outside and look at some trees.
Can you tell which one is the biggest?
Try to wrap your arms around the
trunk of the tree. Try to stretch your
arms in the air as tall as the tree. Is
the tree bigger or smaller than you?

Trouble in the Hen House

Circle the picture that is smaller than the first one.

Try It!

What words do people use to describe sizes, shapes, and weights? Think of as many words as you can, such as **long**, **short**, **light**, and **heavy**.

Home Sweet Home

This ▲ is a triangle.

Color two triangles green.

Try It!

Fold a piece of paper in half. Draw a dotted line diagonally from a corner on the fold to a corner on the edge. Cut along the dotted line. When you unfold the paper, it will be in the shape of a triangle. Try cutting different lines to change the shape.

The Hen House

7
seven

Circle 7 s.

Circle 7 s.

Try It!

How many crayons do you think you can fit on your hand without them falling off? Test your guess.

Counting Seven

The Pond

8 •••• ••••
eight

Circle 8 s.

Circle 8 s.

The Fairgrounds

9 ●●● ●●● ●●●
nine

Circle 9 🚩 s.

Circle 9 🍦 s.

Try It!

Ask a grown-up to help you type the numbers from 1 to 9 on the computer. Print out the numbers, and then practice reading them.

27

Counting Nine

Calling All Sounds!

Say the names of the pictures.
Circle the picture whose name begins with the same sound as the first one.

E eggs

F fish

G goat

H horse

Try It!

Play animal alphabet with a friend. Name an animal and ask your friend to think of something else whose name begins with the same letter as the animal's name.

28

Animal Babies

Circle the baby that belongs to each mother.

Try It!

Some baby animals have very different names from their parents. A baby turkey is called a poult. A baby rabbit is called a kit. How many baby animal names do you know?

Have You Any Wool?

These   are the same size.

Circle the pictures that are the same size.

Try It!

Gather four fruits or vegetables. Line them up according to size. Which is the largest? Which is the smallest?

Shaping Up

This [ ] is a rectangle.

Color two rectangles **orange**.

Try It!

Use blocks and a board to build a ramp. Roll a toy car down the ramp to see how far it goes. Add more blocks to the ramp and roll the car again. Does it roll the same distance?

Saying It Loudly

Say the names of the pictures.
Circle the picture whose name begins with the same sound as the first one.

I ice cream

J jelly

K kite

L leaf

Try It!

Think of words that start with each letter of the alphabet to make up silly animal descriptions. For instance, "giddy goose," "messy mouse," or "purple, picky pig."

32

Great Shapes

Color the picture.

▭ s **red**

△ s green

◯ s yellow

▢ s blue

FARM FUNNIES

Why did the chicken cross the playground?

To get to the other slide!

33

Shapes

Matching the Tracks

Draw lines to match the animals to their prints.

Try It!

Place one of your shoes on a piece of paper and trace its outline. Trace the outline of someone else's shoe on another piece of paper. How are the outlines different? Can you tell which outline is your shoe's?

People on the Farm

Circle the picture that is different.

Try It!

Draw a picture of something make-believe. Make up a story that tells what happens in your make-believe place.

Shoo, Crows!

Use a  to measure each scarecrow.

How many s tall is each one?

1. ☐

2. ☐

3. ☐

Try It!

Ask a grown-up to cut a piece of string about 12 inches long. Look around your home and guess which things are the same length as the string. Then use the string to check your guesses.

Matching the Sounds

Say the names of the pictures.
Circle the picture whose name begins with the same sound as the first one.

Tea Time

2 is more than 1.

1 is less than 2

Circle the set that has more.

Try It!

Suppose you wanted to bake two cookies for each person in your family. How many cookies would you need to bake?

©School Zone Publishing Company

Animal Families

Draw lines to help the animals find their homes.

Try It!

You can make a bird's nest. First, roll some clay into a ball. Press your thumb down in the center to form the nest's shape. Then find things to make the nest cozy, such as feathers, yarn, or bits of fabric. Stick them in the clay to finish your nest.

What Comes Next?

Color the next one.

Try It!

Arrange jelly beans in a pattern, such as two red, one orange, two red, one orange. Ask a friend to continue the pattern. After a few patterns, you can eat the jelly beans!

Sound Roundup

Say the names of the pictures.
Circle the picture whose name begins with the same sound as the first one.

Q quilt

R rabbit

S socks

T turkey

Try It!

Go on an alphabet hunt! Pick a letter of the alphabet. Then look in an old newspaper or magazine to find names that begin with the letter. Circle the names with a marker or crayon.

Cookie Match

Draw lines to match the cookie cutters to their cookies.

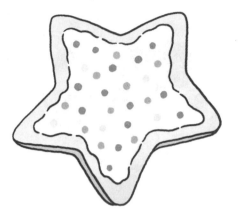

Try It!

Find pairs of objects that are exactly alike, such as mittens, socks, and hair bows. Place the objects on the floor and mix them up. Then match the pairs together again!

43 Matching

Which House?

Draw lines to match the animals to their houses.

FARM FUNNIES · FARM FUNNIES ·

What is the strongest animal?

The snail. It carries its house on its back.

Picking a Pen

Draw lines from the sets of sheep to the correct pens.

8   3   5

DUCK - Sheep

Try It!

Play an imaginary animal game. Combine two animal names into one. For instance, a puppy combined with a hamster could be a pupster. What are the silliest combinations you can think of? Draw the wackiest animals.

45   Number Recognition

How Many Legs?

Try It!

Challenge a partner while traveling by car or bus. Count all of the legs you see on people, dogs, and birds. The winner is the person who counts the most legs.

Color one box for each animal.

Animals with 2 legs						
Animals with 4 legs						

Apple Trees

Draw s on each tree.

Draw as many s as you want.

How many s?

What kind of apple isn't an apple?

A pineapple.

FARM FUNNIES • FARM FUNNIES •

Counting and Addition

48

©School Zone Publishing Company

Try It!

Walk around your neighborhood and collect leaves from various trees. Sort the leaves by shape, color, or size. How are the leaves different? How are they the same?

How many 🍎s? ☐

How many 🍎s in all (🌳 + 🌳)? ☐

Counting and Addition

Where Does It Belong?

Draw lines to where the things belong.

What Do They Eat?

Draw lines to match the animals to what they eat.

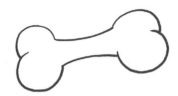

Try It!

Play a rhyming game. Open a magazine or a book with pictures. Point to a picture and say its name. Then say as many rhyming words as you can, even if they are nonsense words. For example, if you see a tree, you could say **bee, key,** and **glee!**

Look at All the Babies!

Count how many there are.
Write the numbers.

S

S

S

S

Try It!

Suppose a farmer could raise an imaginary animal, such as a dragon or a unicorn. What kind of food would the farmer provide? Where would the animal live? Would it need special care?

Count how many there are.
Write the numbers.

53

Counting

How Plants Grow

Write 1 by what happened **first**.
Write 2 by what happened **next**.
Write 3 by what happened **last**.

54

How Does a Goose Grow?

Number the pictures in order from 1 to 5.

Try It!

Cut apart a three-panel or four-panel comic strip. Then ask a friend to arrange the pictures in an order that makes sense.

Story Order

Counting the Animals

Count how many are on both pages.
Circle the numbers.

🦆 S   4   5   6

🐸 S   1   2   3

🦋 S   6   7   8

Count how many are on both pages.
Circle the numbers.

1   2   3

2   3   4

5   6   7

Try It!

Make the sounds of different animals. Moo like a cow. Snort like a pig. Cock-a-doodle-do like a rooster.

57

Counting

Listen Up!

Say the names of the pictures.
Circle the picture whose name begins with the same sound as the first one.

U up

V valentine

W wagon

X x-ray

Y yo-yo

Z zebra

Is It Alive?

Circle 4 living things.

People, animals, and plants are living.

Try It!

What if animals wore clothes? Draw some animal clothing, such as a scarf for a giraffe or shoes for a chicken.

Living and Non-Living

Solving the Riddles

✔ the animal that answers the riddle.

I am white.
I have feathers.
I lay eggs.
Who am I?

I am fat.
I am black and white.
I have a short tail.
Who am I?

I am small.
I have long ears.
I have a short tail.
Who am I?

I am brown.
I have a short tail.
I give milk.
Who am I?

Animal Characteristics

What Goes Together?

✔ the picture that makes sense.

🐝 is to 🍯 as 🐴 is to _____.

🚗 ☐   📬 ☐   🏚️ ☐

🦆 is to 🏞️ as 🐦 is to _____.

🛝 ☐   🌳 ☐   🏠 ☐

🍕 is to 👧 as 🌾 is to _____.

🐱 ☐   🐴 ☐   🦆 ☐

Why Did This Happen?

✔ the picture that shows why.

YOU'RE #1!

Great Job!

This is to certify that:

(first name)

_____

- -

_____

(last name)

_____

- -

_____

has completed **Preschool Scholar**
from School Zone Publishing Company.